A HARVEST *of* COLOUR

Saving Cornfield Flowers in
North East Yorkshire

IAN CARSTAIRS

HALSGROVE

First published in Great Britain in 2006

Title page photograph: Corn marigold. *Dedication page photograph*: Forget-me-not.
Index page photograph: Scarlet pimpernel.

British Library Cataloguing-in-Publication Data
A CIP record for this title is available from the British Library

ISBN 1 84114 484 3

HALSGROVE
Halsgrove House
Lower Moor Way
Tiverton, Devon EX16 6SS
Tel: 01884 243242
Fax: 01884 243325
email: sales@halsgrove.com
website: www.halsgrove.com

Printed and bound by D'Auria Industrie Grafiche Spa, Italy

Contents

DEDICATION

*This book is dedicated to the memory of Anya McCracken (1954–1998)
and David Arnold-Forster (1956–2002), both of whom played
significant parts and who would have loved the results.*

Foreword

By Sir Ben Gill

Former President of the
National Farmers' Union

A New Role for Farmers

What a formidable task! It is one thing for plants to survive naturally, another entirely to try to manage and reintroduce them by design, while at the same time efficiently producing food crops.

What sets this unique project apart from many nature conservation initiatives is that it is working with farmers, not to create nature reserves, but to secure a place for the plants of arable fields within the agricultural landscape. For this, it relies on the interest and goodwill of the farming community.

As more farmers participate, the risks to these vulnerable plants will diminish and the areas maintained for them on the less productive parts of each farm, if repeated across the countryside, would soon build for them a more secure future.

With changes to the emphasis of farm support, from production to land and environmental management, there are new opportunities to make such a project worthwhile for any arable enterprise. I sincerely hope that the message will spread, so that farm and land managers can play their part and that the day will come when the Cornfield Flowers Project will no longer be needed.

That will be the true measure of success.

Ben Gill
Easingwold,
North Yorkshire

Introduction

What Nan Sykes, a local naturalist, found when she surveyed the wild plants of the North York Moors National Park was very disturbing. So many of the once-common plants of arable fields had gone.

In August 1988, she wrote to the late Anya McCracken, of the Park's Advisory Services:

> I have been looking extensively at arable land throughout the Park. The conclusion is that apart from a few common species, the arable plant flora has practically disappeared. Therefore, I feel it is all the more urgent to take steps to retain the few which do remain.

A Harvest of Colour – Saving Cornfield Flowers follows the extraordinary efforts of a small number of people, inspired by Nan and her colleague, Chris Wilson, a farmer, to take up the challenge and to do something about it.

Through a series of photographs, it explores the past, present and future of these increasingly-rare inhabitants of our countryside, and charts the successes and sometimes the setbacks of our unique Cornfield Flowers Project.

Nan Sykes.

Chris Wilson.

Opposite: *A field full of poppies by the roadside is guaranteed to cause motorists to stop and take a photograph.*

It also celebrates the plants themselves, with their often delightful names, such as weasel's-snout, shepherd's-needle and Venus's-looking-glass. Some, such as corn marigold and poppy, create a riot of colour, whereas many others are so tiny you would scarcely notice their existence. And who wouldn't be excited by the sight of the intense blue of cornflowers, set against the mellow colour of the surrounding crop?

Aesthetics are important, but they are just a part of the story. Plants are the bed-rock on which all other living things depend, and increasing the variety of arable plants will help other wildlife as well.

Sometimes the desperate search for long-lost plants seemed an impossible task. But with skilled eyes scanning the ground, almost miraculously, one-by-one survivors would be discovered, their seeds collected and grown on.

Nurturing seedlings in the nursery and demonstration area at the Ryedale Folk Museum was not without its headaches; we soon discovered that rabbits, pheasants and slugs could be equally as devastating to the plants in our care as chemical herbicides in the fields.

Like releasing a wild animal to fend for itself, the culmination of the process lies with the reintroduction of our scarce plants back into a working cornfield to fend for themselves. Some cope, others have not fared so well.

But when will the job be done? Well, not yet, by a long chalk. If the only place these plants survive in future is in protected areas, nature reserves or gardens, we will have failed: they have to be able to manage on their own. So, together with an increasing number of farmers, our quest is to ensure they once again become an enduring part of our working countryside. That is our yard-stick for success. This needs to happen not just here in North East Yorkshire, but throughout the country.

It is a vital and urgent task, for we lose the variety of our wild plants at our peril. Not only are they the beginnings of all of our food, be it meat or vegetable, but many have medicinal properties some of which have yet to be investigated.

We therefore hope our project will serve as a test-bed for others to safeguard also the future of arable plants in their areas. Equally importantly, we hope it will encourage wide appreciation that their conservation can only realistically be achieved in the context of modern-day food production, on which we all rely.

And vitally, we hope it will trigger the interest of more farmers to join in, not only to reap the benefits of the new agri-environmental financial schemes, but also to foster pride in the skills needed to maintain these rare and traditional flowers and plants of the fields as a part of successful and profitable farm enterprises. It is on our farmers that these plants depend.

Our aim, of course, is not to try to turn the clock back to the way of farming in past centuries, rather we seek to safeguard the arable plants today within the scope of economically-successful farming of the highest environmental quality.

It is not easy. But, then, no one expected it would be … and if it was easy, none of us would ever be needed.

Without Nan's original work and Chris's tenacity, supported by many volunteers, the Cornfield Flowers Project would not have happened and many of our arable plants would have slipped further towards oblivion.

There is enormous satisfaction in seeing living things rescued 'from the brink'. Once achieved, the challenge is to keep it that way.

Ian Carstairs
Malton 2006

Chamomile shark moth caterpillar on mayweed surrounded by corn mint – one thing depends on another – no food plant, no moth.

PART ONE

The Past – Ups and Downs

One thing affects everything we do in the working countryside, and that is the rocks and the soils they produce. But what we see today in North East Yorkshire has its origins in events in the far distant past.

During late Jurassic times, one hundred million years ago, the whole of the North York Moors lay under the sea. Over the millennia, deposits laid down on the bed of that sea became compressed into rock, eroded by the waves and lifted out of the water by movements in the earth to form the Tabular Hills.

In the fullness of time, these flat-topped limestone hills, stretching 40 miles from Black Hambleton to the sea, would become the prime arable areas of the North York Moors and, in turn, the main home of many of our wild arable plants found today.

But the recent landscape was not always like this. At the end of the last Ice Age in the moors, about 12,000 years ago, the landscape was bare and desolate. As the climate warmed, vegetation re-colonised the barren land. Eventually, almost all of the moors were blanketed in a forest of oak, elm, lime, ash and other trees.

At that time, the plants we associate with arable land did not live in fields, simply because there were none. Instead, their natural home lay in the disturbed soils in other habitats caused,

for example, by land slips and erosion, the uprooting of trees and the activity of animals.

The first people to visit the moors after the ice had retreated were Mesolithic (Middle Stone Age) hunter-gatherers (c.7000 BC), venturing up onto the higher ground on summer hunting expeditions and starting to clear the wildwood by the use of fire. The frequency of the visits increased and by the middle of the Bronze Age (c.1500 BC), human occupation spread across the high ground; settled farming had begun and much of the forest had been cleared.

Above: *Annual plants depend on disturbed bare ground: the blue variety of scarlet pimpernel.*

A modern reconstruction of a hut similar to those which might have once provided homes for Bronze Age people.

With the shift from hunter-gatherers to farmers, in a relatively short time the plants of disturbed ground found a massive increase in suitable places for them to colonise.

But there was a price to pay for Bronze Age society on the tops where the heather now grows. The sandstones which form the main uplands were laid down, not under a sea like the Tabular Hills, but in a river delta, and their soils were thin and poor. With the protective tree cover removed, their goodness was soon depleted and the soil eroded away. Coupled with a marked deterioration in the climate, it was not long before farming on the tops collapsed and the spread of blanket peat began.

It was a different story on the Tabular Hills, where our Cornfield Flower Project is based. Here, the natural fertility of the better quality soils made it a prime place for arable farming. And, from the distribution of hand-operated stone querns used to grind corn which have been discovered, the extent of arable farming in the Iron Age (from c. 600 BC) seems to have been much the same as it is today.

We can find other clues of the likely extent of arable crops in the area. Over the whole of north-east Europe, including Yorkshire, old villages of tightly-grouped houses, much like Hutton-le-Hole and Appleton-le-Moors (probably dating from the twelfth century AD), are a sign of an historic connection with arable farming. Living close together, inhabitants would help each other by sharing the tasks, animals and equipment needed to cope with the scale of work to manage the crops in the open fields.

Management of the land would not have changed much over the centuries and it is likely there would have been little vari-

Opposite: *A familiar sight 60 years ago, but now very rare indeed.*

ation in the pattern of land use and crops from year to year. Yields would have been low and competition from arable 'weeds', a significant problem.

From the seventeenth century, the narrow strip-farmed open fields were progressively enclosed, communal use diminished and power to use and manage the land in a more organised way passed to individual farmers.

Sometimes the enclosure of the former open fields took place by agreement, but often, in the eighteenth and early nineteenth centuries, it was forced through by Acts of Parliament. The amalgamation of the narrow strips of the open fields into larger units also paved the way for more efficient use of horse-drawn and, later, steam and petroleum powered equipment.

As if enclosure was not dramatic enough, other truly revolutionary changes were on their way.

From the 1730s onwards, Lord Charles 'Turnip' Townshend, introduced the concept of rotation in Norfolk. Instead of repeated use of the land for the same crop, management – known as a four-course rotation – now involved cyclical changes alternating between cereal production, root crops, short-term clover-rich grassland and fallow. This improved the quality of the land, increased yields and brought with it more competition for the wild plants growing in these fields

The onset of the decline of arable plants was now just around the corner. This really began in the mid-nineteenth century, when the first chemical herbicides were introduced. Coupled a few decades later with improved seed-cleaning techniques, made possible through the capabilities of seed-sieving in steam-powered threshing machines, technology was beginning to give the farmer the upper hand over the age-old adversary – arable weeds – in his fields.

Modern technology has increased yields out of all recognition.

Improvements to machinery and the efficiency of herbicides, and the impacts of artificial fertilisers carried on apace throughout the twentieth century. Driven by memories of World War II and food rationing, maximising food production was rightly seen as an urgent national strategic need. And there is no doubt that British farmers have been hugely successful in responding to society's demands.

That success has delivered high yields from fields now cleaned of the plants which once competed with the cereal crops, or jammed-up farm equipment. But, today, there is a new emphasis in the demands of society as we seek to address the impact of our modern way of life on the environment and living systems of which we are a part.

Yes, we need the highest quality food, but we also need to keep the environment in good order too. Providing space for wild plants and animals alongside modern agriculture is a new challenge, one which we must grasp if they are to survive.

Nan Sykes's survey of the plants of the Moors showed just how close we have come to eradicating the plants of arable fields. It was a wake-up call, and it came just in the nick of time.

Arable plants – an annual cycle

Most arable plants are annuals. They germinate, flower, set seed and die, in a yearly cycle. Some germinate in autumn, others in spring. All need the land to be disturbed regularly for the right conditions to flourish. Some seed is very short-lived, for example corncockle, whereas that of other plants, such as the poppy, may lie dormant in the ground for many years. Arable plants also include a range of grass species. But it is the cornfield flowers which people most readily recognise.

In the right conditions, seed which has lain dormant for many years can germinate with dramatic effect.

The Tabular Hills

So-called for their flat, table-like tops, these limestone hills with their steep north-facing escarpment are formed from layers of rock which once covered the whole of the North York Moors.

The big freeze
Between 100,000 and 12,000 years ago, the North York Moors were gripped in the last Ice Age.
This aerial photograph taken above Snilesworth Moor looking west, creates an impression of
what it might have looked like. But today it is fog, not ice, which fills the Vale of York.

The trees return

After the ice retreated, as the climate warmed, vegetation colonised the bare ground.
Eventually, trees covered almost the whole of the landscape of the North York Moors,
except, perhaps, for the very highest ground, which might have been open grassland.

Over-exploitation
Bronze Age burial mounds are found throughout the Moors. Standing today in open heather-covered countryside,
they are testament to the communities which once lived on the tops, but who were forced to leave
when the land was exhausted and could no longer support farming.

A breadbasket across the millennia
The soils of the Tabular Hills sloping to the south (left), are ideal for arable farming,
and have been used this way for 2,500 years.

Back-breaking work

These two illustrations from the medieval calendar of a psalter (c.1250–75) show reaping the fields with a sickle in July (left) and threshing with a flail in August (right). They bring home the nature of the back-breaking seasonal tasks faced to manage crops before the days of mechanisation.

Re-organising the landscape
In medieval times, the open fields were worked communally. But, between the seventeenth and nineteenth centuries, large areas of the countryside were enclosed and rigid geometric field patterns were laid across the land to bring the fields into individual ownership and occupation.

Helping one another
Old villages of closely-grouped houses, such as here at Hutton-le-Hole, are often associated with arable farming areas, in which the tasks and equipment needed to work the fields would be shared.

Horse-power
Until the twentieth century, animals provided the main motive power for ploughing the fields,
as the historic photographs by Frank Meadow Sutcliffe on pages 21–23 show.

Traditional harvest
Stooks of corn stand drying in the fields, waiting to be threshed to remove the grain.

A well-earned rest
Workers take a break from their labours at harvest time. The man on the right is seated
on a 'rat trap' reaper, a predecessor of the combine harvester.

More horse-power
In the late nineteenth and early twentieth centuries, steam, which had revolutionised travel on the railways, now heralded the start of mechanisation of agriculture. Steam-powered traction engines with belt drives could be used to power farm machinery, such as threshing machines.

Progress drives on
The arrival of the internal combustion engine, light and versatile in comparison with steam-driven
vehicles and machinery, greatly increased the power-to-weight ratio of agricultural equipment.
Kevin Simms drives a vintage small tractor from the Ryedale Folk Museum's collection.

Massive horse-power – many functions
A modern combine reaps, threshes and sieves the grain and with a chopper on the back, can even finely chop up
the straw in a single pass. A far cry from the labours of the fields in the past.

Aerial mist
The use of chemicals to protect crops and increase yields, occasionally applied from the air, plays an important part
in the scale of production achieved today, but their effect is so extensive that many wild plants
and other wildlife find it difficult if not impossible to survive.

Plants – vital for life
Plants are the only living things on earth that convert the
sun's energy into food. This orange-tip butterfly is not
feeding, but roosting on a shepherd's-purse plant at night.

PART TWO

The Present - Winds of Change

In 1998, one of the tasks facing the North York Moors National Park Authority was the preparation of a Park-wide Plan. Among other things, this plan set out the priorities for work in the Park in the coming years.

The timing could not have been better. Recognising the importance of the results of Nan Sykes' survey, the conservation of threatened plants of arable fields was added to the target list of management tasks.

The opportunity to take action came sooner than anyone expected. Over the years, the trustees of the Carstairs Countryside Trust (CCT), had also been looking to help arable plants. In another coincidence, a small botanical group in Sleights, near Whitby, of which Chris Wilson was a member, had become particularly interested in finding the places where rare plants grew. Almost without trying, the pieces dropped into place.

The plan was straightforward: the Park Authority would grant-aid the Trust to buy an arable field, for use as a repository for rare plants while Nan and Chris, helped by Rona Charles, the Park's ecologist, with their combined store of knowledge and network of contacts, would handle the finding and nurturing of the target species.

But where should the land be, how should it be managed, would it be financially viable, and where would we collect seed?

Initially we had hoped to run the land under a traditional four-course rotation, the management regime within which the

Rona Charles inspects the nursery.

plants once thrived. Calculations by Ron Foster, a well-known Rosedale farmer and a founding supporter of the project, suggested that while such management could be viable, it would only work if a tenant could be found who was willing to undertake such a complex operation. Although the four-course rotation would have been best for the plants, the risks associated with embarking on this approach were considered to be too great.

With Ron's help, a less ambitious plan was devised; half of the field would be farmed for commercial production and the other half farmed without the use of sprays and fertilisers, to favour the wild arable plants. However, as it turned out, we would soon change this to working the field as a single unit, but, without the use of sprays and fertilisers, in broad 12–32m-wide headlands round the edge.

The right location was vital. The field needed to lie on the limestone soils of the Tabular Hills which stretch across the south of the National Park. It was also a prerequisite that the land should have been in long-term arable cultivation.

Determining which species would be appropriate to find and increase was also quite a task. However, hours spent by Nan in libraries and second hand bookstores seeking old and out-of-print publications eventually revealed information about the plants which grew here a hundred years ago, before the decline truly set in (see information box p35–36).

It was a first principle of the project that all seed gathered should be of local provenance or as near local source as possible. However, some of the plants recorded a century ago had now not been seen in the area for many years.

Rona and Nan came up with a pragmatic approach. The area of search would cover the whole of the Park as well as the Vale of Pickering, the northern parts of the Yorkshire Wolds and the Howardian Hills.

While this covered a large area, logic dictated that since arable seed would have been transported considerable

Nan Sykes sets out on a plant-hunting expedition.

Growing-on seedlings at Thorn Park Farm.

distances among grain in the past, working over a wider area than the Park, which after all, is merely an administrative concept, was a reasonable and practical approach to take.

For plants which were completely absent, such as cornflower and corncockle, a species-by-species decision would be taken, depending on the source, before bringing it in from elsewhere.

Initially, finding a single field to buy proved problematic. But luck was once again on our side. David Barber, an agricultural consultant and contact of Nan, had a client who wished to sell one and, in April 1999, the Trust acquired a 25-acre (10 ha) field at Silpho, not far from Scarborough. Lying on the top of a hill overlooking a deep valley and with wide vistas, not only was it ideal, it was also idyllic. For the first few years, Pat Foxton, who sold the field to the Trust, tenanted the land, as we took our first cautious steps into the reality of harmonising commercial farming and the conservation of arable plants.

It had been intended that a small part of the field would be used as a nursery, where volunteers could grow-on seed in controlled condi-

Young plants go on the move to Silpho.

tions. But Silpho is remote and exposed and proved not to be a practical proposition for this work. However, all was not lost. Far from it.

Nan had been a long-time volunteer at the Ryedale Folk Museum, where she tended the cottage garden. Her links with the museum enabled her to encourage the then curator, Martin Watts, to agree that the nursery might be in the Museum's vegetable garden. More than that, Martin arranged that there should also be a small demonstration field where old varieties of cereal crops could be grown and the surplus seed of the arable plants introduced.

It fitted in well with the spirit of a 'Folk Musuem' and provided many benefits: a delightful location for volunteers to work in; a secure place to grow on seedlings and, most importantly, a show-case for the project, which the public could enjoy. It also brought the support of Kevin Simms, Yvonne Morley and the infectious enthusiasm of Mike Benson, the manager, as the project became an established part of the museum's activities.

Slowly, the seed resource and number of surplus plants from the nursery increased, so more could be introduced at Silpho and into one or two other locations on the land of sympathetic farmers.

In 2002, John Simpson, a Harwood Dale farmer, took over the tenancy at Silpho from Pat Foxton with Ian Kibble, a trustee of CCT, acting in a liaison role. Without John's co-operation, delivering the management we need would be difficult. And John himself now has arable flowers on his farm, where visitors to his bed-and-breakfast can hear about the work he is doing.

Our intention is that the arable plants will become self-sustaining in the wild. Perhaps not enough time has elapsed yet, but it has been a slow process at Silpho. On the up-side, the results in the demonstration field at the Museum have been spectacular and the enthusiasm of the visiting public, a joy. And with the help of Spaunton Estate we have expanded our nursery and trial work into The 'Mushroom field', about two miles away.

Now, six years into the project, the volunteers, including Jill Magee, Gill Pullen, Julia Lockwood and John Ramsdale, have already helped to pull several plants, such as corn buttercup, red hemp-nettle, shepherd's-needle and Venus's-looking-glass, back from near extinction in the area.

Their unstinting efforts at planting out, weeding, seed collection and harvesting, along with the work of unseen volunteers who keep an eye out for plants as they go about the countryside, have created a spectacle which is a delight to behold, spangled with the colours which were once common throughout the countryside.

The photographs on pages 42 to 86 celebrate a range of the plants with which we have worked. The images are not intended to be a field guide to the plants, there are other publi-

Counter-measures to pheasant and rabbit attack.

Opposite: *Nan Sykes monitors the sole corn buttercup plant known from Yorkshire.*

cations which do this job admirably. They are simply an artistic reminder of the variety and beauty of cornfield flowers which still deserve a place within our countryside.

Today, many of these plants are so uncommon that organisations such as Defra (The Department of the Environment, Food and Rural Affairs), which assisted the project with advice, have in turn used the demonstration field to help their own staff to recognise them.

Paradoxically, the more successful the project has become, the more anxious it has made us. At present, it would only take one disastrous year of extreme weather, determined attack by other wildlife, germination failure or accidental use of herbicides in the wrong place, to set back seriously the achievements, perhaps even returning the plants to the highly precarious position of a few years ago.

As the first years of the new millennium unfold, almost miraculously, the wind of change in agriculture has started to blow in our direction. The review of the EU Common Agricultural Policy has shifted financial support from crop production onto looking after the land.

Many of the plants might seem more secure as a result of the project, though the achievement is in itself tiny in comparison with the scale of the problem. However, they are all growing in just a small number of places under our control. To reduce the risks to the plants, the next step is to increase seed as rapidly as possible and then encourage more farmers to join in and work with us.

Only by achieving sustainable populations in a wide range of locations can we begin to feel that the future might be truly a little brighter for them. As you will see in part three, this is now underway.

The public find out about the Project at an open day.

Wild pansies flourish in the museum field.

The Target Species

From research carried out at the start of the project, a range of arable plants known to have grown locally at the beginning of the twentieth century was identified. From the original list, only one of the species which we have encouraged, has failed to survive – pheasant's-eye. Others, such as field gromwell and mousetail, have yet to be found in our area, but we are growing them on from seed acquired elsewhere, so that volunteers will know what they look like and therefore what to look for. Several of the plants, such as black bindweed, fool's parsley, red dead-nettle, redshank and mayweed came of their own accord and reappear without the need for re-sowing.

Some plants, notably broad-leaved dock and creeping thistle, always reappear despite being hoed out each year, and they need to be controlled.

As so many plants have different local names, the botanical name for each is included to identify clearly the precise plant species involved.

Bird's-foot	*Ornithopus perpusillus*
Black-bindweed	*Fallopia convolvulus*
Bugloss	*Anchusa arvensis*
Corn buttercup	*Ranunculus arvensis*
Hairy buttercup	*Ranunculus sarduous*
White campion	*Silene latifolia*
Night-flowering catchfly	*Silene noctiflora*
Corncockle	*Agrostemma githago*
Cornflower	*Centaurea cyanus*
Common Cornsalad	*Valerianella locusta*
Cut-leaved crane's-bill	*Geranium dissectum*
Dove's-foot crane's-bill	*Geranium molle*
Cut-leaved dead-nettle	*Lamium hybridum*
Henbit dead-nettle	*Lamium amplexicaule*
Fiddleneck	*Amsinckia intermedia*
Field penny-cress	*Thlaspi arvense*
Flixweed	*Descurainia sophia*
Sharp-leaved fluellen	*Kickxia elatine*
Common fumitory	*Fumaria officinalis*
White ramping-fumitory	*Fumaria capreolata*
Field gromwell	*Lithospermum arvense*
Large-flowered hemp-nettle	*Galeopsis speciosa*

Cornflower.

Fiddleneck.

Red hemp-nettle	*Galeopsis angustifolia*
Field madder	*Sherardia arvensis*
Corn marigold	*Chrysanthemum segetum*
Mayweed	*Tripleurospermum inodorum*
Corn mint	*Mentha arvensis*
Mousetail	*Myosurus minimus*
Treacle-mustard	*Erysimum cheiranthoides*
Field pansy	*Viola arvensis*
Wild pansy	*Viola tricolor*
Parsley-piert	*Aphanes arvensis*
Fool's parsley	*Aethusa cynapium*
Pheasant's-eye	*Adonis annua*
Scarlet pimpernel	*Anagallis arvensis*
Common poppy	*Papaver rhoeas*
Long-headed poppy	*Papaver dubium*
Wild radish	*Raphanus raphanistrum*
Shepherd's-needle	*Scandix pecten-veneris*
Dwarf spurge	*Euphorbia exigua*
Corn spurrey	*Spergularia arvensis*
Stork's-bill	*Erodium cicutarium*
Small toadflax	*Chaenorhinum minus*
Venus's-looking-glass	*Legousia hybrida*
Weasel's-snout	*Misopates orontium*
Field woundwort	*Stachys arvensis*

Field Pansy.

Venus's-looking-glass.

The initial list involved a realistic assessment of the species which we considered it might be possible to find. With experience and greater knowledge it became clear that there was a reasonable chance of finding several additional species, as follows:

Smooth cat's-ear	*Hypochaeris glabra*
Bur chervil	*Anthriscus caucalis*
Narrow-fruited cornsalad	*Valerianella dentate*
Round-leaved fluellen	*Kickxia spuria*
Fine-leaved fumitory	*Fumaria parviflora*
Corn parsley	*Petroselinum segetum*
Prickly poppy	*Papaver argemone*
Green field-speedwell	*Veronica agrestis*
Grey field-speedwell	*Veronica polita*

Prickly poppy.

The Silpho field
The headlands which are managed without chemicals or artificial fertilisers to benefit our
arable plants have been harvested. The rest of the field awaits the combine.

Setting the seed and the scene
Plants are first grown on in the vegetable garden at Ryedale Folk Museum to multiply the seed resource
before being introduced as either seed or plants into the demonstration field at the museum and,
when there is sufficient, into the Silpho field, or those of other farmers.

Opposite: **Ryedale Folk Museum – the cottage garden**
A better setting and association for the nursery and demonstration field would be difficult to imagine.

Preparing the ground
Ploughing the demonstration field with the Museum's 'Fergie' tractor in preparation for seed sowing.

Painstaking work
Managing the nursery is all done by hand, with a labour-intensity
reminiscent of farming in the medieval fields.

A thrill to behold
The public are captivated by the way fields used to look and by experiencing, first-hand, plants which hitherto few had heard of and which even fewer had ever seen.

Triticale
Triticale, a long stiff-strawed hybrid between wheat and rye, was chosen as the host crop for the flowers, especially as pheasants and rabbits, the bane of the arable plant-grower's life, are not too keen on it.

Bird's-foot
A tiny treasure found in sandy fields between Staxton and Knapton.
Its flowers are no bigger than a ladybird.

Bugloss
Even hungry slugs avoid the coarse bristly foliage which
protects these delicate, deep blue flowers.

Corn buttercup
Tiny hooked spines on the seeds help the plant to spread on the fur of mice and voles and give it
the name of 'devil's coachwheel'. Another name is 'watchwheels'.

Hairy buttercup
Locally, as difficult to find as the hairs on its foliage are to see, despite its name.

White clover
Commonly, a plant of grasslands, which also appears on arable land, though for several reasons it is not welcome in either when the aim is nature conservation.

Corn marigold
Our vibrant display of 'golds', as we often call this plant, originates
from four plants spotted and saved from a local field.

Corn mint

You can sometimes have too much of a good thing. Only a few plants were discovered
in the wild, but once we'd got it, corn mint spread vigorously and would
have smothered everything else if not controlled.

Common cornsalad
There are a number of species of cornsalad which might be found locally, but it is almost impossible
to tell the difference between them until the plants set seed.

Corn spurrey
Small is indeed beautiful with this starry-flowered plant. But, as here, they are
reluctant to open unless the sun is shining and seeing
them will have to wait till another day.

Corncockle
With seeds almost as big as a grain of wheat, this dramatic and easy-to-grow
plant fell victim to modern seed-cleaning techniques, and is
now virtually extinct in the wild in this country.

Cornflower
'Bluebottle' was said to "trouble the cornfield with its destroying beauty".
The native cornflower is dark blue – garden varieties are
larger-flowered and come in a variety of colours.

Fiddleneck
A yellow-flowered forget-me-not which was accidentally introduced to this country
with seed from America. It can be very prolific in sandy soil.

Field gromwell
The nearest plants we could find were a few in Hampshire, 300 miles (480 kms away).
Our specimens are only grown for demonstration, so people know what
to look for locally. The small clusters of seeds are distinctive.

Field madder
One of the few wildflowers found in our Silpho field before we started introductions. It seems able
to survive many modern farming techniques, perhaps because its low-growing,
carpeting form poses little threat to commercial cropping.

Field woundwort
Still survives in small pockets in the wild locally but it is often
overlooked due to its unobtrusive and rather dull flowers.

Forget-me-not
We're never likely to forget these charmers. This adaptive group of plants has evolved a look-alike
species to suit almost any habitat – hence at least 12 different forget-me-nots grow in our area.

Sharp-leaved fluellen
Chris found this growing in a barley field. On approaching the owner
for permission to remove it he was told, "Only on the
condition that you take the bloody lot!"

Common fumitory
Well named, as it is still quite plentiful in the wild, unlike other fumitories which are now very scarce.

White ramping-fumitory
We had searched in vain for this more showy white and wine-coloured fumitory,
until it was found by volunteers scrambling around field edges near the sea.
We then realised its distribution is largely coastal.

Large-flowered hemp-nettle
This flashy-flowered hemp-nettle far outshines its more sombre relatives,
but is very choosy where it grows, preferring damp peaty soils.

Red hemp-nettle

Now you see it – now you don't! Found in a number of places, from which it then
disappeared, the very rare 'star-of-our-show' has now been discovered near
Thixendale in perhaps the largest concentration in England. It is, however,
reluctant to sustain itself in our nursery without gathering seed and
resowing them each year to ensure its survival.

Small toadflax
The flower is very tiny, but definitely worth a hands-and-knees job to look closely.

Mayweed

Because its leaves resemble fennel, this widespread plant became known as 'dog finkle'. Actually, some jumped the fence into the vegetable garden and fooled the gardeners into thinking it was fennel, and they carefully hoed round it.

('Dog' means common or everyday, and is nothing to do with canines).

Mousetail
The demonstration specimen came from further afield than our search area, so we are still
looking for seed of this well-named tiny plant which used to frequent
local fields but has not been seen for some time.

Night-flowering catchfly
Pollinated by moths, its flowers only open at night. During the day, due
to its rather pathetic, crumpled appearance, it is easily overlooked.

Field pansy

Heartsease, just one of its common names, encapsulates in a word the enchanting
simple beauty of this small and still widespread cornfield flower.

Wild pansy
Larger and more colourful than heartsease, the wild pansy
is more difficult to find and is quite rare in the wild.

Field penny-cress
Well-named after the shape of its large seeds, but in truth it has no
known use – perhaps not worth tuppence, according to Chris.

Common poppy
The shallow, bowl shape of the flower aptly gave it the local name of 'cuprose'.

Long-headed poppy
It is easy to see the long seed pod when the flower is over, but unless you
break a leaf stem, you will not know if it is the rare yellow-juiced
variety or the widespread white-juiced poppy.

Redshank

An aggressive spreading plant which is still plentiful in the wild. Pheasants like to feed on it, but we would like to be rid of both in our nursery and demonstration field.

Scarlet pimpernel
Lives up to its name of 'poor man's weatherglass' by only opening in bright light.
It also occasionally produces brilliant blue or shell-pink flowers.

Dwarf spurge
Very much the rarest of our spurges growing locally,
and difficult to find in the wild now.

Shepherd's-needle
It's easy to see how it got its name. In the flowering season, both the
flowers and the long seed heads can be present on the same plant.

Stork's-bill
The delicate pink flowers are followed by distinctive seed heads, shown opposite.

Stork's-bill
Named after its seed heads, which resemble a stork's head.

Thorow-wax
Although a plant was found locally in the wild, there is some uncertainty as to whether
it was a garden escape, which means we will not use the seeds for reintroduction.

Treacle-mustard
A tallish, ungainly plant with very small flowers and one of the
rarer crucifers (four-petal, cross-shaped flowers).

Venus's-looking-glass
This small elusive plant, related to bellflowers, only opens in sunlight.

Weasel's-snout

How weasel's-snout plant got its name is a mystery, though perhaps it is because it looked like a weasel's nose poking out of the vegetation. Also known as lesser snapdragon.

White campion
Known in the Yorkshire Wolds as 'soldiers buttons', it is found on the
fringes of fields and occasionally among the crop.

Seed collection
Julia Lockwood undertakes the time-consuming job of seed collection.
All cannot be collected at once as the seeds of different species ripen at
different times. It is a true labour of love, but a very rewarding one.
Seed is kept in paper rather than plastic bags to prevent it from sweating.

Harvest time
The crop and flowers are mown as the public enjoy the Museum's traditional harvest day.

The day's work done
Gill Pullen gets the ice creams after a long day's work collecting seeds.

Somewhere to celebrate
The delightful Manor House at the Museum – a great place for our end of season get-together.

PART THREE

The Future - Broadening the Horizons

For the past 50 years, national and European funding for farmers has been focussed on supporting production. This has been highly successful in driving forward efficient farming and increasing yields in the United Kingdom, though at times gave rise to overproduction, where payment was guaranteed, even if the produce was not needed.

On January 1, 2005, all this changed. With the review of the Common Agricultural Policy, the link between payment and production was severed. Instead, farmers are now supported for managing their land for the benefit of the environment while producing their crops.

Importantly, in addition, farmers can join Environmental Stewardship Schemes, successors to the Countryside Stewardship initiatives which had paved the way for environmental work on farms. These offer extra payments for specific conservation works. On arable land, the options to help wildlife include providing beetle banks to encourage beneficial insects, leaving stubble for winter bird feeding areas and creating plots for skylarks and other ground-nesting birds.

Of particular interest to the Cornfield Flowers Project are the options connected with helping arable plants. These options involve maintaining field headlands without the use of sprays and fertilisers, or maintaining uncropped cultivated field margins.

Decisions wrought in the corridors of power in Brussels have now presented the best opportunity for the future of arable plants in recent years. At the same time, the Project has been handed a vital, though unexpected chance to unite and expand its work with mainstream agricultural business in a way we could barely have dreamed of at the outset of our 'insurance policy'.

However, making the most of the opportunity to encourage wider involvement by farmers, and increasing the seed resource to service them needed far more time and sustained effort than the small group of volunteers could possibly muster.

Following successful bids to the Heritage Lottery Fund and the National Park's Sustainable Development Fund Chris Wilson took over the running of the project on a part-time professional

Chris Wilson, rather pleased with his find of sharp-leaved fluellen – "not extinct, just not seen for a long time".

basis for five years. And we are sure there can be few farmers who have turned their enthusiasm for plants that, in Chris's own words "contaminated the crops with colour" in the past, into a focus of diversification for their own business in the future. Not only does Chris provide the capacity, but also as a farmer he speaks the language of other farmers and when urgent land management tasks loom, he can switch hats and has the skills and machinery to deal with them.

Our exit strategy – to put it into ghastly modern jargon – is to have at least 50 participating farmers whose land has a range of soil conditions in which the plants can flourish in a self-sustaining cycle, at sufficiently varied locations for the species to survive the odd disaster here and there.

The message is beginning to spread and today the number of sites involved has increased. Some examples are shown on pages [91 to 93]. But we look forward to more.

The only qualification needed for newcomers is a commitment to make the project work; the only obligation, in the true fashion of everything which has been achieved to date, is based on co-operation, trust and shared enthusiasm between colleagues for the task ahead.

If at the end of the project our goal is achieved, then perhaps we can say, maybe not that the whole job is done, but at least our part of the job has been completed. The whole job can only be a success when there is a network of places across the country where arable plants flourish and can sustain themselves.

We are encouraged that, given a fair wind, it could work. Why do we think that? Well, two reasons. First, Chris refuses to accept the word extinct, preferring to describe plants in such a potential predicament as "just not seen for a long time". And he is right. With refusal to accept that a plant has gone, and the keen, experienced eyes of his band of volunteers searching, it is surprising what has been found.

Secondly, perhaps the best reason for optimism and the last word should be with Stephen Gibson, a farmer from Terrington in the Howardian Hills.

"As a commercial wheat grower with a lifetime interest in the countryside, I am enjoying learning about and encouraging cornfield wild flowers on field margins which are not viable for modern agriculture. I even have a blue version of scarlet pimpernel on my land."

Change is underway – a corner is being turned.

Countryside Stewardship and Environmental Stewardship Schemes

The Countryside Stewardship Scheme (CSS) was introduced in the early 1990s to reward farmers for carrying out landscape, historical and nature conservation work on their farms and where appropriate to provide access for the public. Instead of being paid to maximise production, payments were made to support less viable, but nevertheless valuable management of the land of public benefit and for any capital works associated with it. In 2005, following a review of the EU Common Agricultural Policy, Countryside Stewardship was replaced by the Environmental Stewardship Scheme (ESS), with similar aims, but which has two tiers – Entry Level, open to all farmers and land managers, and Higher Level, which is targeted at specific local opportunities. Payments are made towards both.

Farther Afield

As the Cornfield Flowers Project expands a number of farmers and landowners have joined in to work with us. Here they explain about their farms and conservation work.

John Simpson
Keasbeck Hill Farm
Harwood Dale

Keasbeck Hill Farm covers 200 acres, under arable, sheep and cattle, with hay for sale and the farm's own use. Diversification projects include bed-and-breakfast accommodation, a tea room and a nursery selling pot plants, including an increasing number of wildflowers.

John said: "The farm has been in the Countryside Stewardship Scheme for 13 years. We have several ponds with a selection of local waterside plants, and a wildflower meadow which I created. It's nice when people can enjoy our achievements, and we've set out a concessionary footpath which gives access to many parts of the farm.

"For the last three years I've also been the tenant of the Silpho field, mixing commercial farming with the special management the arable plants need."

Stephen Gibson
Birkdale Farm
Terrington

Peter Hutchinson
Spikers Hill Farm
West Ayton

Birkdale Farm covers 300 acres – 250 of which are arable and 50 pasture, grazed by sheep. Other enterprises include a holiday cottage and fishing lakes.

Stephen said: "The farm has been in Countryside Stewardship Scheme for nine years. There are 20 acres of grass margins and almost four acres of arable margins are being created, along with 12 acres of wood pasture using acorns from the famous Mowbray Oak at Slingsby.

"Five acres are down to wild bird seed mix, and 25 acres are in a rotating fallow option, with 16 acres of arable reverting to grassland and 3000 metres of newly-planted hedge with trees, berry-bearing bushes and a series of wet scrapes for birds.

"A bird count is carried out every two months, with 98 species now recorded including some unusual records – for example, hoopoe, stonechat and quail. Barn, tawny and little owls all nest on the farm.

"We already have some rare or unusual arable plants such as smooth tare, treacle-mustard and hairy buttercup. We've also introduced a number of species including red hemp-nettle, shepherd's-needle, field gromwell, sharp-leaved fluellen, corn-flower, corn marigold and Venus's-looking-glass.

"As well as all the plants and birds, the site of the lost medieval village of Mowthorpe is also on the farm."

Spikers Hill covers a total of 570 acres, which are down to arable, beef cattle, sheep and lambs. There are also two holiday cottages.

Peter commented: "The farm was entered into the Organic Countryside Stewardship Scheme in 2002 and all produce, including the corn, is now sold as organic.

"The scheme includes arable margins which the project has been helping to manage. These margins produced the first self-sustaining re-introduction of red hemp-nettle in 2003 and again in 2005. Other plants growing in the margins include fine-leaved fumitory, prickly poppy, grey field-speedwell, small toadflax and Venus's-looking-glass, from which the seed for the Cornfield nursery was collected.

"Other notable wildlife on the farm includes tree sparrows, barn owls, lapwings, skylarks and grey partridge.

"Because of the organic status of our farm, we take care not to introduce any aggressive plants which might be difficult to control without the use of herbicides. It's just a matter of being sensible."

John Middlewood
Glebe Farm
Potter Brompton

Chris Wilson
Thorn Park Farm
Hackness

Glebe Farm is in the Vale of Pickering and covers 350 acres. The soils are sandy with some peat. The farm is mostly in arable cultivation with a few sheep, 500 free-range chickens and some turkeys. Other enterprises include a farm bakery run by John's daughter, Sally. Hen's eggs are either used in the bakery or sold.

The farm has been in the Countryside Stewardship Scheme for five years, and a number of margins for arable plants and arable reversion to pasture have been established.

"Our four acres of set-aside land has been especially rewarding," said John. "We've found that the management suppresses grasses in a way which benefits many arable plants including some rarities for the area, such as smooth cat's-ear, bur chervil, bird's-foot, hare's-foot clover and knotted clover.

"Our arable margins also have a wide variety of other uncommon plants including prickly poppy, common cudweed, stork's-bill, fiddleneck, bugloss, viper's bugloss and broad-fruited cornsalad. In addition, red hemp-nettle, shepherd's-needle, small toadflax , Venus's-looking-glass and corn buttercup have been introduced by the Project."

Thorn Park Farm covers 180 acres, which is mostly improved grassland supporting an intensive dairy herd of over 100 cows. A further 90 acres, a third of which is arable, is at Seamer, four miles away. Other enterprises include running the Cornfield Flower Project.

Chris said: "Most of our fields at Hackness are surrounded by ditches in which many plants can be found. The ditches contain white-clawed crayfish and are occasionally visited by otters. Adjacent grassy areas are home to a thriving population of voles and shrews. Barn owls use a nest box provided by the Hawk and Owl Trust, and we've planted three areas of woodland and gapped-up and laid the hedges.

"The land at Seamer has been in Countryside Stewardship for 12 years, and is now a designated site of importance for nature conservation. This land includes the site of the old Seamer Manor House, which benefits from the Stewardship historical options and includes open access. A large part of the farm is the former site of the long-drained Seamer Mere, where ponds have been created and become naturally stocked with many species of coarse fish. Birds of the mere area include reed bunting, water rail, cuckoo, kingfisher and many species of warblers.

"Three and a half acres of the arable land is is being reverted from arable to meadow, with a further 20 acres managed to leave over-winter stubbles to encourage English partridge and skylarks."

Finding Out More

A good, comprehensive book containing a wide range of information about arable plants is:

Arable Plants – a field guide by Phil Wilson and Miles King Published by WILDGuides Ltd, Parr House, 63 Hatch Lane, Old Basing, Hampshire RG24 (2003). www.wildguides.co.uk ISBN 1-903657-02-04

Useful addresses

North York Moors National Park Authority
The Old Vicarage
Bondgate
Helmsley
York
YO62 5BP

Telephone: 01439 770657
e-mail: general@northyorkmoors-npa.gov.uk
Website: www.moors.uk.net

Ryedale Folk Museum
Hutton-le-Hole
Nr Kirbymoorside
York
YO62 6UA

Telephone: 01751 417367
e-mail: all_addresses@ryedalefolkmuseum.co.uk
Website: www.ryedalefolkmuseum.co.uk

Wild plants and the law
Please remember it is against the law to intentionally uproot a wild plant without the land-owner's permission. For some extremely rare plants it is also illegal for anyone to pick their flowers or uproot and destroy them.

National nature conservation initiatives
The Cornfield Flowers Project fits in with a number of national national nature conservation initiatives, notably the UK Biodiversity Action Plan (BAP) (www.ukbap.org.uk), as well as contributing directly to the objectives of the Cereal Field Margins Habitat Action Plan and the red hemp-nettle and shepherd's-needle Species Action Plans. In the North York Moors National Park and Ryedale, the Project makes a significant contribution to local Biodiversity Action Plans, in which threatened arable flowers are a focus.

ACKNOWLEDGEMENTS

The Cornfield Flowers Project - Who made it happen

The Cornfield Flower Project is managed by a partnership of The Carstairs Countryside Trust (Ian Kibble and Ian Carstairs), Ryedale Folk Museum (Kevin Simms) and the North York Moors National Park Authority (Rona Charles).

They are helped by a Steering Group, comprising: Yvonne Morley (RFM Education); Naomi Jones and Nigel Boatman (Defra Central Science Laboratories); Jill Magee, Ron Foster (farmer and countryman); Nan Sykes (plant specialist) and Chris Wilson (plant specialist and Project Co-ordinator).

The project could not have been developed without the extensive assistance of a wide range of other people, including: Lesley Blainey (Defra, Rural Development Service (RDS)); Neville Turton and David Barber (Agricultural advisors); Richard Watson (solicitor – Crombie Wilkinson); John Simpson (farmer), and most importantly Jill Magee, Gill Pullen and Julia Lockwood among others, who, stoically, in the face of the worst that Nature could throw at them, nurtured seedlings though to flourishing flowers in the fields, and the other volunteers who scanned the countryside for plants and seeds.

Finally, special thanks must go to Patrick Ferguson, who organised the illustrations for this book and played a significant part in its completion, and to Roly Smith, editoral manager for Halsgrove, whose encouragement ensured that the project is recorded for posterity.

The transition of Chris Wilson from key volunteer to professional Project Co-ordinator engaged through the North York Moors National Park, to manage the expansion phase of the cornfield flowers work on behalf of the partnership is supported by the Heritage Lottery Fund and the North York Moors National Park's Sustainable Development Fund.

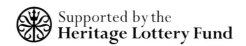

Photographs and illustrations

APS (UK) – Beverley/Neil Mitchell: 37. Ian Carstairs: Front cover (right), 6, 7 *bottom*, 10, 12-20, 26-29, 30 *top*, 32, 39, 42, 43, 45, 46, 48, 50-52, 59-66, 68-71, 74-84, 89, 93 *right*, 96. Patrick Ferguson: Outside covers, title page, dedication page, 7 *top*, 25, 34-36, 41, 47, 49, 53-58, 72, 73, 85, 87, 88, 96. John Lawson: Front cover (left), 24, 86. Jill Magee: Front cover (centre), 29. Sophie Rogers: 38. Nan Sykes: 33, 44, 67. Chris Wilson: 8, 9, 31, 33 *top*, 36 *bottom*, 40. Peter Wilson: 30 *bottom*.

The photographs by Frank Meadow Sutcliffe Hon. F.R.P.S. (1853–1941) on pages 21-23 are Copyright ©The Sutcliffe Gallery, 1 Flowergate, Whitby, YO21 3BA by agreement with Whitby Literary and Philosophical Society. Further information about the gallery and Sutcliffe's work is available on the gallery's website www.sutcliffe-gallery.co.uk or by telephoning: 01947 602239.

The medieval illustrations on page 18 are reproduced by courtesy of Corpus Christi College, Oxford and The Bridgeman Art Library, references MS CCC 285 f.6 and MS CCC 285.6v.

Plant index